FINANCIAL LITERACY:- A WAY TO FINANCIAL WELL BEING.

RAUSHAN KUMAR & PAVNESH KUMAR

Made with ♥ on the Notion Press Platform
www.notionpress.com

Dedicated to our Parents and Friends, for their motivation, encouragement, and support.

Contents

Preface

Financial products have experienced phenomenal growth as an alternative to traditional investments as a result of the development and growth of the Indian economy and the subsequent expansion of the financial markets. Financial literacy education must be provided at all levels for the countries due to the rising complexity and variety of financial products, the shifting of responsibility for social security from the government to individuals, and the growing significance of retirement planning. This is because individuals with low financial literacy are unable to make wise financial decisions and are therefore unable to choose the most suitable investments. It might be viewed as the initial stage towards the development and alleviation of poverty in developing nations. The majority of countries today place a high priority on financial literacy. Literally speaking, financial literacy refers to the capacity to make wise financial decisions by applying knowledge and abilities. It has a significant impact on a nation like India because it is thought to be crucial for the advancement of financial inclusion and, eventually, financial stability. Financial literacy is the capacity to comprehend how money functions in the real world, including how someone makes money, how they manage it, how they invest it, and how they give money to others in need. Financial literacy is the combination of ability, information, attitude, and conduct those results in appropriate use of financial services and relevant financial decisions.

Making informed financial judgements has become crucial on a global scale in the quickly evolving financial markets of today. This is particularly true for women, who confront difficulties like: longer life expectancies than males; Gender salary discrepancies; and Career interruptions because of maternity leave and other reasons.

Acknowledgements

We are incredibly grateful to "Bhagwan Shri Ram" for providing us opportunity and the willpower to accomplish this book as successfully as possible. Before we get started, We would like to say a few words of gratitude to everyone who help and mentoring us through the stages of this book completion. We owe these people the utmost appreciation.

We would like to express our sincere appreciation to everyone who helped us to write this book; without their active participation, the book could not have been finished within the allotted time. We cannot explain how grateful and humble we are to everyone, who helped us turn these ideas—which go beyond the level of simplicity—into something solid.

No endeavour, regardless of degree, can be successfully completed without support and advice from parents and friends. We would like to express our gratitude to our parents for helping us to make this book distinctive.

Last but not the least we dedicate this book to every source of information that served as our inspiration.

Our heartfelt apologies to anyone whose contribution, we may have accidentally missed. We want to let them know that their input is just as valuable and important.

Abbreviations

AI:- Artificial Intelligence

ANZ:- Australia & New Zealand Banking Group Limited

BC:- Business Correspondent

CEO:- Chief executive officer

CFPB:- Consumer Financial Protection Bureau

CBSE:- Centre Board of Secondary Education.

FEPA:- Financial Education Programme for Adults

FETP:- Financial Education Training Programme.

FACT:- Financial Awareness and Consumer Training.

FSDC:-Financial Stability and Development Council

GDP:- Gross Domestic Product

GoI:- Government of India

INFE:-International Network on Financial Education

IRDAI: - Insurance Regulatory and Development Authority

LIC:- Life Insurance Company

MSSP:- Money Smart School Program

NPCI:-National Payment Corporations of India

NSFE:-National Strategy for Financial Education

NCFE: - National Centre for Financial Education

NCFE:- National Centre for Financial Education

OECD: - Organization for Economic Co-operation and Development

PMJDY:- Pradhan Mantri Jan Dhan Yojana

PF:- Provident Fund

PFRDA:-Pension Fund Regulatory and Development Authority

RBI:- Reserve Bank of India

SCORES:- SEBI Online Complaint Redressal System

SHGs:- Self Help Groups
SEBI:- Securities and Exchange Board of India
UN:- United Nation
UK:- United Kingdom
USA:- United States of America

CHAPTER ONE

WHAT IS FINANCIAL LITERACY?

Financial Literacy, Covering the basics: - In academic and political arena, financial literacy has gained many advantages and has taken variety of meaning over the period. It has used to refer knowledge of financial products, financial services, financial concepts, financial management, financial planning, and financial decision making. It also influences people to save, invest and process to manage their financial resources as well as play a role in influencing financial institutions because financial literacy affects people's investment decision that how much risk and returns are available in the economy. In short financial literacy affects resource allocation in the economy that influences in both short term as well as long term economy.

Financial literacy is a component of financial activities that can increase the expected life of an individual from financial consumption that can enhance financial well-being. A person who is financially literate and smart may predict the future financial outcomes.

India is a fastest growing economy in the world which focuses on inclusive growth with sound and stable financial system. The government has accordingly prepared National Strategy for Financial Education (NSFE) under the Financial Stability and Development Council (FSDC) that can cover the need of all the sections of the society.

1.1 Definitions: -

According to *RBI India*, Financial literacy defines understanding financial products and effective use of financial services by every section of the societies. With increasing knowledge regarding financial literacy, one can cope up with bad debt and can planning about smart money management.

OECD defines financial literacy as the process by which an individual improves the level of understanding and develops their skills about financial well-being to become more aware about the financial risks and opportunities and make a rational decision of financial service.

According to *World Bank* financial literacy is a concept of financial awareness and knowledge of various financial services, institution and skills and ability to manage the money.

Robert T. Kiyosaki defines financial literacy in his book "Rich Dad, Poor Dad" that A person can be highly educated professionally successful, and financial illiterate.

According to *Jump$tart*, a US nonprofit organization on financial literacy defines financial literacy as a ability to use one's financial resources over lifetime financial security in effective and efficient manner.

According to *US financial literacy and Education Commission 2007*, financial literacy is an ability to use financial services effectively and efficiently for financial well being.

According to *US CFPM*, Financial education is an antidote for financial capabilities.

According to *National Bank of Hungary* financial literacy is a level of financial knowledge and skills that enables an individual in identifying financial information to make conscious and prudent decision.

According to *National Centre for Financial Education (NCFE)* financial education is a combination of awareness, skill, attitude, behavior and knowledge of financial education to make sound and smart financial decisions to achieve individual financial well-being.

1.2 Financial Literacy, An International Context: -

In USA, the US Federal Reserve Board founded Jumpstart coalition for personal financial literacy in early 2000s to survey the financial literacy among high school students biannually. Recently US Senate Committee on Banking, Housing and Urban Affairs conducted hearing into state financial education and literacy and US Department of Treasury created financial literacy and education commission with special focus on improving financial education in a country.

In UK, Financial Services Authority called a meeting of industry leaders and consumer activist to develop an organization to enhance the education of financial education, consumer education and financial advice. The Authority had developed a statutory body called "Consumer Financial Education Body" in 2010 later called The Money Advice Service. Personal Financial Education Group and Citizen Advice Bureaux are several other agencies of UK to increase the level of financial literacy among the people.

On the other side of the Pacific, a Japanese consumer finance study found that more than half of adult respondents knew nothing about financial products, and 71% of respondents had limited knowledge of equities and bond investments. An examination of young Koreans‘ knowledge of economics and finance in 2000 by the Jump$tart coalition revealed that they performed no better than their American counterparts, with the majority obtaining failing grades. Once more, a link between family income, level of education, and kids’ performance on the financial literacy test was found to be positive.

Although people’s understanding of finances is lacking, they also frequently have more confidence in their skills than is justified. For instance, a 2003 Commerzbank AG survey in Germany indicated that while 80% of respondents felt confident in their knowledge of financial matters, just 42% were able to properly answer 50% of the survey questions. Australia, the United Kingdom, and the United States all exhibit comparable trends. In fact, consumer overconfidence in their financial literacy may discourage them from seeking out expert guidance, thereby expanding the "knowledge gap."

1.3 Financial literacy in India:

India has a large young population and this demographic advantage of young population can be achieved by India by spreading large number of financial education program. Since large number of financial stakeholders are involved in spreading financial literacy but the level of awareness is not at par. A board of NSFE is constituted to ensure that level of financial education must be improved.

NSFE is a document that intends to support the vision of Government of India and financial sector stakeholder like RBI, SEBI, IRDAI and PFRDA in nationally co-ordinated approach to financial education programme. NSFE 2020-2025 is prepared by National Centre for Financial Education (NCFE), a not-for-profit company registered as section 8 of Companies Act 2013.

The Survey report on National Strategy for financial Education 2020-2025, was compiled by a multi stakeholder and that approach is to creating financially aware and empowered India. The report recommends adoption of 5 C's approach for dissecting the term financial education.

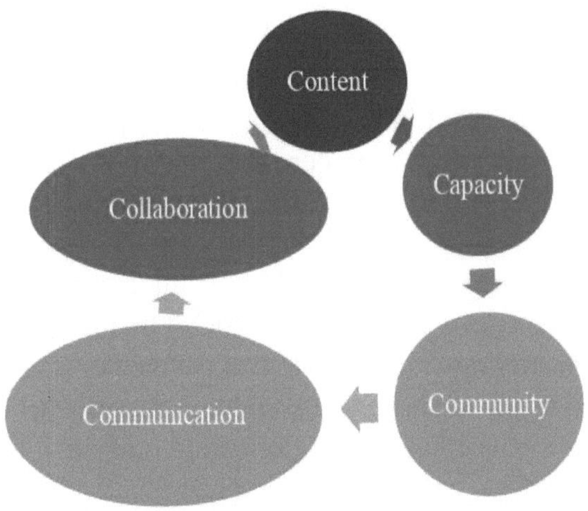

- **Content:-** Content means to add knowledge of finance and financial education in our curriculum. As we see there has been very less finance related things available in our textbooks. So, financial literacy content for School level, College level, University level, Women, Entrepreneurs, Senior citizens, illiterate and disabled person must add in curriculum. There should be also proper training establishments available for financial education.

- **Capacity:-** The financial stakeholder and intermediaries must be work for increasing financial education between un-served sections of the societies. Recently, RBI appoints many intermediaries for measuring and improving financial education in rural and semi urban areas. BCs are the one of the intermediaries of RBI, who has appoint to educate people about financial education.

- **Community:-** Community means leveraging the positive effect of financial literacy between the community. Community is a approach to bring discarded people under the umbrella of financial literacy.

- **Communication:** - Communication means to flow a proper and clear communication of financial education through proper channel. Use of technology, mass media and digital media in to disseminate the financial literacy and education. Misinformation about financial educations must be stopped and appropriate communication strategy should be adopted to achieve the target of inclusive growth.

- **Collaboration:-** Collaboration is a multi stakeholder approach and there should be collaboration between different financial stakeholder of RBI. The stakeholder should also suggests adoption of robust Monitoring and Evaluation framework to assess the progress made by Financial intermediaries.

India has jumped in financial education since Pradhan Mantri JanDhan Yojna savings account has launched. According to RBI, Financial Education is higher among men as compared to women in India. A survey conducted revealed that 29% of males polled qualifying on all fronts as compared to females it is only 21%. When it compared to 2013, there has been some improvement in financial literacy among males and females.

Chart 1:- Percentage of Population Crossing the Minimum Threshold Score Gender-wise

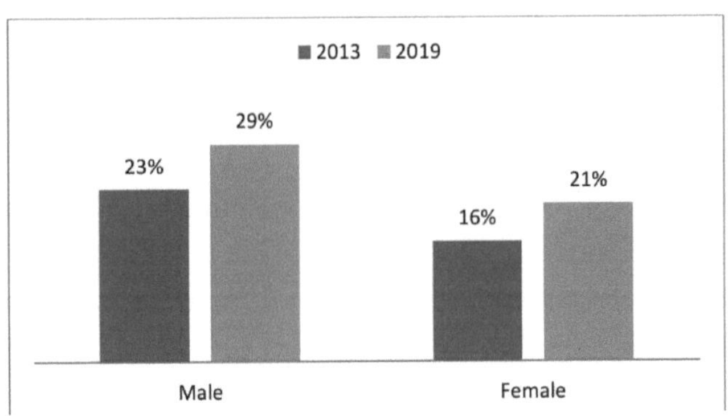

Source:- NSFE (2020-2025)

Chart 2:- Percentage of Population Crossing the Minimum Threshold Score Zone-Wise

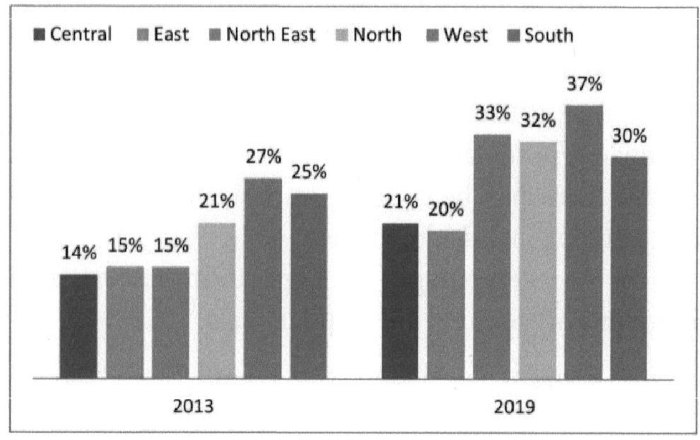

Source:- NSFE (2020-2025)

NSFE has divided Indian region into six parts to measure the level of financial awareness. The six regions are as followed Central, East, North-East, North, West, and South. Financial literacy and financial education are higher in West followed by North-East. The Central India has performed poor in financial awareness.

Chart 3: Percentage of Population Crossing the Minimum Threshold Score Occupation- wise

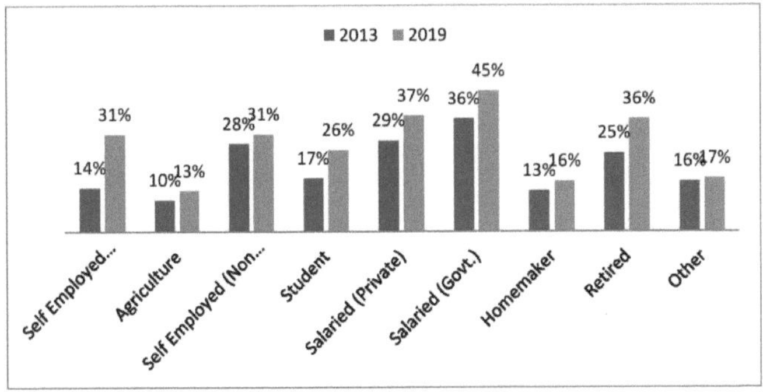

Source:- NSFE (2020-2025)

1.4 Benefits of Financial Literacy:-

Since People will start making financial decisions beginning as early as they are in school and college level, so it is important to give them informed and sound decision of financial education. They are taking decision in their school loans, Car and Bikes loan and having debit card and credit card. So, good financial decisions through financial literacy programs give them informed and smart decisions.

- Financial Literacy assist an individual in rational decision on complex financial services and products.
- It improves economic condition of disadvantaged groups.
- It improves economic insecurity of disadvantaged sections of the society.
- Financial literacy provides optimum utilization of own finances and that promotes in economic development.
- Financial literate people can mitigate the financial risk such as purchasing insurance, diversifying assets, and

accumulating saving.

- Financial literacy makes people as a responsible citizen such as pay taxes on time, timely clearance of bills and avoidance of over-indebtness.
- Financial literate people can make smart saving decisions and compare financial products and services and give advice on financial matters.

1.5 Financial Literacy and its components: -

Financial literacy along with financial inclusion plays a vital role in providing empowerment among the youths that can contribute in overall economic and financial stability. Financial literacy is a matter of concern in public policy field that can provide welfare through better decision making. So, measures of financial literacy are very much valuable for government and policymakers to check the level of financial inclusion among the consumers.

The term financial literacy, financial education and financial knowledge are often used by scholars to differentiate the definition but the objectives of all are almost same. The level of financial literacy depends on level of financial education and financial knowledge. There is no standardized test to measures the level of financial literacy. One can check the level of financial literacy on the basis of financial behavior, financial attitude, financial influences and financial knowledge. It is very well known that governments around the world are implementing effective policies for financial education to improve the financial literacy among the people. So, measuring financial literacy involves measuring the skills, attitudes, behavior, knowledge and awareness of people while making financial decisions.

According to recent survey, India consists of 17% of total world's population and 24% of Indian population is financially literate. Although there has been increased in the understanding of financial concepts but still mass population of India suffers.

Components of financial literacy

There are three components of financial literacy as per (OECD-INFE):-

1. Financial Knowledge.
2. Financial Behavior.
3. Financial Attitude.

1.5.1 Financial Knowledge: - Financial Inclusion without financial knowledge has no meaning and will not fulfill the idea about risk and benefit associated with financial services. Many people living in semi-urban and rural are unaware about financial products and services and they failed to make a rational decision about savings, borrowings, expenditure, and investments. Financial knowledge means understanding of day-to-day financial concepts and evaluates financial risks and situations.

1.5.2 Financial Behaviour:- Financial behavior means to study of money management, credit meet, financial planning, saving, investment, and risk associated with day to day financial activities. Hence, financial behavior means understand the overall impacts of financial decisions and take a right decision for financial well-being.

1.5.3 Financial Attitude:- Financial attitude means people attitude towards financial knowledge and inclination towards financial matters. It provides an ability to plan about saving and investments. Financial attitude can be achieved when financial education betters. Hence, financial attitude is a state of mind of people about finances.

CHAPTER TWO

FINANCIAL LITERACY, WHY IT MATTERS?

2.1 Overview: -

Ultimately, the idea of financial literacy is about to fulfill the criteria of financial inclusion and promotes in inclusive growth of any country. There are large ranges of economic choices are available in the market and people should make a rational decision about their resources rather than simply based current decisions. A new rational perspective needs to be required for smooth consumption of people's income.

Financial literacy is important for an individual for their welfare and managing financial affairs. It is the first step towards achieving the dream of financial inclusion. It is considered an important subsidiary for promoting financial inclusion. The aim of financial literacy is to facilitate financial inclusion through easy access of literacy about financial services. The basic financial knowledge of Indian people is really worrying and it is much worse, when it comes to Indian women. According to survey conducted by S&P, more than 75% of Indian adults do not understand the basic financial services and more than 80% of Indian women are financially illiterate.

The idea of financial literacy has increased over the past decade to protect the consumer rights and financial well-being. It refers to make informed judgments and effective decision regarding money management. Mostly rural and semi-urban sections of the society have still dependent on informal sources of income due to unavailability of fund and hence they must depend on moneylenders and landlords. Due to poor education about financial services, larger shares of the population have still in search of easy access of finance. Thus, financial literacy promotes and understands the importance about savings and money management.

2.2 Financial Literacy around the world: -

A survey conducted by S&P global financial literacy survey was conducted across 140 countries. A survey tested the knowledge of four financial concepts like numeracy, risk diversification, inflation, and compound interest (saving and debt). According to the survey two thirds of adults worldwide are not financial literate. In India, data shows that 76% of adults in India are not financial literate and only 24% of Indians responded about financial concepts like numeracy, risk diversification, inflation, and compound interest (saving and debt).

According to the survey, more than 1, 50,000 representatives from 140 countries were selected and the target population was 15 years and above. Most of youths from major advanced countries like Canada, France, Germany, Italy, Japan, UK and the USA are financially literate. In contrast, 28% of adults are financially literate from major emerging economies like BRICS (Brazil, Russia,

India, China, and South Africa).

% of adults who are financially literate

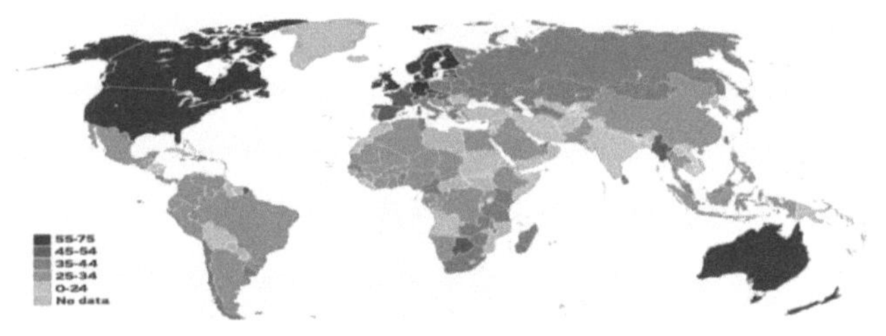

Source:- S&P Global FinLit Survey

In ***North America,*** it makes it clear that, financial knowledge increases over the time. The US (57%) and Canada (68%), in contrast to Mexico's 32%, are both in the lower half of the global average. Greenland was unable to provide data for the researchers.

South American financial literacy statistics are depressing. The best rates are in Uruguay and Chile with 45% and 41%, respectively, although most regions have rates between 21% and 30%. There are undoubtedly several historical justifications for this gap, but Nicaragua's (20%) particular concern stands out as a source of concern. Its score is the lowest in all Central and South America, excluding the Caribbean, and it reflects the dire circumstances there.

But nowhere else in the world has such a wide range of financial literacy as in ***Europe***. Scandinavian nations with high scores, most notably Norway and Sweden (71% each), serve as the continent's fulcrum. On the Financial Literacy Survey, northeastern European nations seem to fare the best, and the situation gets worse the further south one looks. Portugal does poorly, with a 26%, ranking last in all Western Europe. While no country east or south of Hungary scored over 50%, the Eastern Bloc has numerous glaring and startling issues.

Africa performs the worst of all the continents on several different indicators of economic growth and development. Only one nation, Botswana, surpasses the 50% mark, with most nations falling between 31% and 40%. Somalia has the lowest rate of financial literacy on the entire continent at 15%. Western Africa, where Sierra Leone is at 21%, is not much better off.

Similar issues exist in ***Asia and the Middle East*** to those in Africa. The two countries at the very bottom of the list, Yemen (13%) and Afghanistan (14%) aren't the only ones in the teens. Several nations had dismal outcomes, from Kyrgyzstan (19%) through Nepal (18%), Bangladesh (19%), and Cambodia (18%). Given that it has the second-largest economy in the world, China's score of 28% was shocking. However, we believe that Myanmar and Bhutan, where an amazing 50%+ of the population is financially educated, are the most intriguing outstanding nations.

Finally, ***Oceania*** isn't a surprise. ***New Zealand*** (61%) and ***Australia*** (64%) are tied for the top rank, but the Financial Literacy Survey was unable to gather sufficient data from any other nation in the region.

2.3 Financial Literacy, Why it matters for India?

There is a common myth in India that people who 'literate' and 'rich' is also "financially literate." But the data shows that the condition of financial literacy in India has been worrying as compared to rest of the world. According to Standards and Poor Financial Survey, India is a home for 17.5% of world population but 76% of the adult population does not understand financial concepts.

In India, Financial Literacy has not in the priority list like any other developed nations. People in India mostly invest in short term plans and physical assets which give lesser benefits and it does not help much in economic growth. Lack of poor understanding about financial knowledge leads to poor financial investment and decisions. As compared to India, most of the developed nations give topmost priorities to the financial literacy programme. They believe that people who have financially literate make better financial planning and turn financial resources in maximum benefit.

2.4 Major areas of financial literacy and why do we care about?

2.4.1) Diversification in assets portfolios: - If individual or households are financially literate then they are more likely to plan for retirement. They may hold different types of assets. Evidence says that Dutch households hold more stocks, good knowledge of finance and control over expenses due to sound financially literate.

2.4.2) Awareness in borrowing decisions: - If an individual is financial literate then they are capable of sound borrowing decision. Individuals with lower financial literate, tend to borrow at higher rate of returns. For an example people of developed countries have particularly engaged in credit card borrowing. If people are financial illiterate then credit card borrowing scores are poor. Hence financial literacy is needed for good borrowing decision.

2.4.3) Better allocation of resources: - Financial sounds people are less likely to affect during financial crisis. They are more aware to know about the effective and efficient utilization of resources. A study shows about German households that they are sell their assets at a loss during financial crisis.

2.4.4) Increased saving behavior: - Awareness rate of financial literacy among women are much higher in developing countries with compare to men. Women have lower retirement age than men and they are more likely to increase their retirement age plan. Hence financial education programmes which are specially target to women are more likely to increase immediate action on financial literacy.

Thus, understating about financial principles and concepts can help people in managing financial pitfalls and avoiding financial risks. Financial literacy can also help in budgeting, debt, borrowing, loan etc. So, therefore financial literacy is important because finances are need in every aspect of life and increasing in financial stability will help us to move from thriving to surviving and whatever income earned by an individual will helps people in transforming their lives. So, that financial literacy is matter for us.

CHAPTER THREE

FINANCIAL EDUCATION AND FINANCIAL LITERACY

Financial Education and financial literacy not the same but these are related ideas. By receiving financial education, a person can become financially literate. An individual can achieve financial well-being by using their financial literacy to make good investment decisions. Financial education helps individual to gain the skills needed to choose rational financial products and to take actions that will improve their financial well-being.

According to the Organization for Economic Co-Operation and Development (OECD), financial literacy and education include:

3.1 Financial Education: "The process by which financial consumers/investors enhance their understanding of financial products, risks and concepts, through instruction, information, and/or unbiased advice, develop the confidence and skills to become more aware of financial risks and opportunities, to make informed decisions, to know where to go for help, and to take other efficient actions to improve their financial well-being."

3.2 Financial Literacy: "A collection of awareness, information, skills, attitudes, and behaviours required to make wise financial decisions and eventually attain individual financial well-being."

3.3 Financial Behaviour: Having the ability to comprehend the total effects of financial decisions on one's circumstances (i.e. family, person, society, nation) and to choose the decisions on financial management, safety measures, and chances for budgeting.

3.4 Financial Education, Financial Literacy, and Financial Behaviour:

Indians tend to have conservative views on financial behaviour, which leads them to put all their financial eggs in one basket, which can lead to significant gains or losses. The nation is known for its propensity for purchasing excessive amounts of gold. Investment choices are not routinely evaluated. Insurance firms are still working hard to persuade people, but people's retirement planning efforts remain lacking. The primary activity in daily life is finance. The business world and high net worth individuals cannot be the only ones managing their health, wealth, and finances. Wealth management differs from financial management in several ways in terms of research and legal considerations, yet it cannot be disregarded when examining the topic of financial literacy.

Financial management skills are not required to manage the pocket change of the underprivileged or those with low incomes. Cash shortages for various emergencies are caused by households' need for liquidity.

Small-scale business capital management is crucial, as is managing the way people will manage their finances in the future, especially the poor and youngsters. The ability to self-manage money for higher education, capital management, health management, company management, and wealth accumulation in the future may be enabled by the people's understanding of the power of compounding. People will learn about the time worth of money by being taught about current and future values.

Additionally, financial literacy includes a wider focus on retirement, insurance, investments, savings, and, if practicable, can extend beyond those areas to include tax and estate planning.

3.5 Consequences of financial literacy:

3.5.1 More Spending, Less Income:

Young people (aged 18 to 24) are progressively overborrowing, which causes financial difficulties because of financial illiteracy or a lack of financial awareness (Atkinson and Kempson, 2004). According to Anthes (2004), employees experienced financial difficulties as a result of blowing their salaries on expensive items like designer clothing and cell phones, even if these purchases were necessary. This was because they were lacking their financial literacy.

3.5.2 Failing to maintain financial records:

Budgeting can alter a person's spending habits by successfully managing their resources. As a result, wasteful expenditure is reduced, and budget maintenance is approached positively (Kidwell and Turrisi,2004). Chen and Volpe (1998) found that students with better financial literacy maintain detailed financial records, showing that those with greater financial literacy regulate their spending habits and decisions in this way.

3.5.3 Failing to take rational financial decision:

According to Chen & Volpe (1998), a person is likely to make poor financial decisions that could result in financial difficulties, such as taking out inadequate insurance, spending more than they earn, and making bad investment choices. According to Garman, Leech, and Garble (1996), bad financial mistakes could be avoided or rectified by giving employees the knowledge and financial counselling that need to handle their money more wisely. Consumers who make poor financial judgements are those who spend more than they earn, do not even keep financial records, and do not plan and carry out regular investment programmes.

3.5.4 Not Planning investment programme:

According to Chen and Volpe (1998) Financially literate students, see financial planning and the implementation of a regular investment programme as a highly significant element of their lives. Those customers who are financially literate makes rational financial decision among those who are illiterate. Most customers lack the knowledge about financial education failed to make wise financial choices.

CHAPTER FOUR

FINANCIAL LITERACY AND WOMEN

4.1 Overview:

There are many remarkable strides for women in today's generation. Women are running more business and engaging the position in Multi-National Companies. According to Fortune Study 2019, there are more women CEO's than men in Fortune 500 companies. Closing the financial literacy education will allow women to support in female entrepreneurs. Both men and women should be collectively participating in economic activities and hence they need to be sufficiently financially literate. This will automatically help in fuel the economic growth by creating women owned business through broad consumer movement.

Women contribute almost half the world population and their participation is must for any country's development. Women are smarter in money management and financial decisions at home and financial literate women must handle the organization in better way rather than financial illiterate. If the women take financial decisions and planning in various sectors of the economy, they will give more contributions in any country's GDP. Financial literate women have the tools to grow their wealth and that will help in close the financial literacy gap.

Women in Semi-urban and Rural areas are ignorant of banking facilities, banking services, day to day transactions, use of debit and credit cards. Awareness of financial knowledge is low in unserved areas. Financial awareness is good only in women of urban areas and high-class societies due to more financial exposure.

4.2 Why Women should be financial literate?

4.2.1 Women mitigate the risk: - Women are risk averse in nature and tend to be always select the low-risk investment because they may be think that their one decision will be going affect the whole families. Women only prefer low risk investments such as Buying and Selling Gold, Fixed Deposit, LIC, Provident Fund (PF) and National Saving Certificate. So, for the good of the family, the decisions of women revolve around the low-risk nature investment.

4.2.2 Women live longer than Men: - According to the World Bank Data, the average life expectancy of any female in India is 70 years while male is 68 years. That means health care and retirement planning is more crucial for women. Women constitute around half the world's population and their participation is must for any country growth. So, Women will need more assistance than men.

4.2.3 Women are smart management planner: - According to the report by Boston College's Center on Wealth and Philanthropy women will have 70% of the nation's wealth by 2030. Women across the world know the excellent management skills for running a house and their family. They are taking all financial decision and investments at their home. So, therefore by 2030 women will have 70% of future wealth and she knows how effective and efficient decisions should be better for any economy.

4.2.4 Women are now multi-tasker:- Women have starting recognizing their true potential in every field and doing work in every field like Politics, Policies, Space, Science, Administration, Academics and many more. So, financial literate women will lift their society in every nook and corner of the field. Financial literate women also take financial leads in various sector of the economy and give contribution to their economy.

4.3 The need of financial literacy programs among women

Financial education for women seems to be a simple solution for policymakers given the convincing evidence of gender inequalities in financial literacy and the fact that they affect women in general. It is difficult to find out appropriate programme for women and it seems to be the important question given the diverse environmental factors and learning preferences. However, there is a significant lack of solid academic research on financial education programmes for women, making it challenging to provide a solution to this topic. (Hung, A., Yoong, J., & Brown, E. 2012)

In accordance Duflo and Saez, 2003 and Bernheim, B. D., & Garrett, D. M. (2003). with previous findings regarding gender, of the financial programmes that were examined by many authors. In contrast to developing nations, most programmes in developed nations concentrated on long-term asset growth, retirement planning, and savings. Evidence from developed nations generally suggests that a variety of financial literacy in relation to retirement savings can benefit through financial education programmes in the workplace, at school, or through other channels for both men and women.

Some of these initiatives, including those for low-income groups, might specifically target women. Women are not specifically addressed for financial education in matched-savings (Individual Development Accounts) programmes in the United States, even though 80% of IDA participants are female and 79% are single. Like this, participants in Australia's Saver Plus programme, which is financed by ANZ and the Department of Families, Housing, Community Services, and Indigenous Affairs, receive matched savings. Although the programme does not specifically target women, an independent evaluation conducted from 2006 to 2009 found that 86.4% of participants were female.

It could be essential to specifically target women through programme and design if they do not respond well to financial education. In fact, following their rigorous analysis of the effects of the financial education programme, The effectiveness of a programme depends on its to be highly targeted, timely, relevant to certain financial activities, and directed at specific sub - groups. By providing close attention to a specific population of interest, several financial education programmes have found success. Hathaway and Khatiwada (2008) Many financial education programmes in developing nations concentrate on removing the obstacles to credit and formal labour force participation that disproportionately affect women. Many microcredit and micro-enterprise programmes for economic development target women primarily or even exclusively. A financial counselling and support component is currently included in many of these programmes, if not all of them, through formal training, peer education, regular meetings, and mentoring. (Halder and Mosley, 2004).

According to Creevey and Edgerton 1997, training within the approach of microenterprise programmes can have independent, positive influences on a person's capacity to generate income in addition to other effects on boosting sociopolitical participation for the women enrolled. The same is true for low-income people in high-income nations

In general, it has been observed that women's financial confidence and knowledge are on par with or lower than those of males. Although certain financial capability/literacy studies indicate that women typically perform better at managing household finances on a day-to-day basis, they still perform poorly in other crucial areas such as planning, product selection, and information retention. These areas are crucial for boosting financial inclusion and entrepreneurship as well as long-term wealth accumulation.

4.4 Status of Financial literacy among women in India

Financial Inclusion and Gender equality have been always one of the sustainable development goals for UN. It has been always a subject of discussion in most of the economies around the world.

Women are almost half of the population in India and therefore for driving an economic growth it is obligatory to empower them. According to a report by the World Economic Forum 2021, India ranked 140th out of 156th countries with 68% gender gap in terms of economic participation. The reason for proximate gap is low financial inclusion across the nation and mostly in rural areas. Financial Inclusion is one of the prominent factors for accelerating economic growth. Since some couple of year, the awareness campaigns and advertising through many channels, we have seen a decrease in gender disparity but at macro level the condition is worse.

Table: Economic Participation and Opportunity Index:-

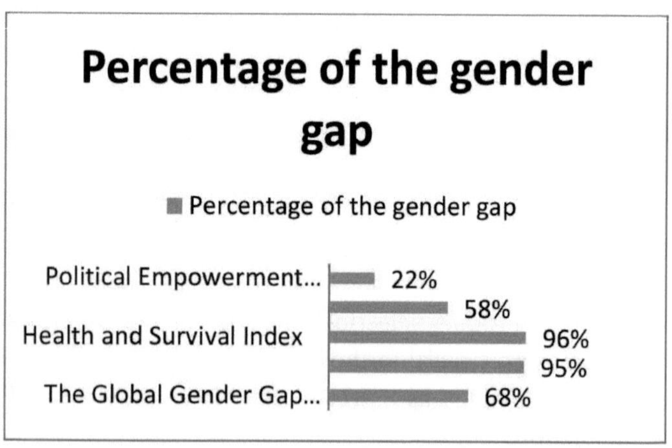

Source:- World Economic Forum, 2021

According to the WEF, 2021 India stands at 151th position in total of 156th countries in the economic participation and opportunity index.

These countries that have smallest economic participation and opportunity gaps are Lao PDR (91.5%), Bahamas (85.7%), Burundi (85.5%), Iceland (84.6%), Latvia (82.2%), Moldova (81.1%), and Sweden (81.0%) and the countries with the largest economic gender gaps are Iran (37.5%), India (32.6%), Pakistan (31.6%), Syria (28.5%), Yemen (28.2%), Iraq (22.8%) and Afghanistan (18%). The exuberant gaps between the two economies are due to inequality between men and women and underrepresentation of women in labour market. Globally, 80% of men aged between 15-64 years and 52.6% of women of the same age group are participated in labour workforce and the data are much lower in developing economies like India and Pakistan.

Besides inequalities in labour force opportunities, financial disparities continue a major barrier among working women and their dependents. When it comes to financial disparities wage gap and income gap between men and women is still a major concern. The ratio of the wage of the women to that of men in a similar position is still approximately 37% and income gap is 51%.

Financial needs generally addressed as a secondary need for women empowerment of in India and especially in rural areas. Although there are many financial literacy programmes and initiatives like Pradhanmantri Jan Dhan Yojana, Sukanya Samridhi Yojna, Mahila e-haat are driven by government of India but many more miles to go. To drive an economy, financial inclusion is a key and that can be achieved through rigorous financial literacy programmes.

India's environment is currently favorable to drive financial literacy programmes. Our first step is to need to invest in financial tools with long term objectives and short-term investment. The journey of financial inclusion is a collective responsibility of state, private players, public bodies, and individual itself that can help to accelerate rate of financial inclusion.

4.5 Importance of Financial Literacy among women in today's life: -

In the 21st century, we see women leading at every possible front. Women are more informed, educated, and rational in their decision-making process. Even today's women are master of multi-tasking and doing careers and households at a time. But despite gaining success from every front, women are still lagging in financial planning. This is one's area through which women are still struggling.

Women contribute around half the world's population and their participation and contribution are must for any country's development. In India, too if the women take the financial leads in various sectors of the economy, they will give a huge contribution in India's GDP. Here are some points that says that financial literacy is much important among the women.

- Financial Literacy will lift their status in the society.
- Financial literacy gives them a confidence in taking independent financial decisions.
- Growth of any country's GDP is not possible without women participation.
- Eradicate ignorance of basic financial services in mainly rural areas like banking transaction and cash deposits.

- Women tend to be risk-averse and prefer low risk investment like

CHAPTER FIVE

FINANCIAL LITERACY PROGRAMMES IN INDIA

5.1 Financial Education Programme for Adults (FEPA):- Financial Education Programme for Adults is a financial literacy programme for creating awareness and empowering them about financial education. FEPA targets mainly adult population about saving and deposit, Debit and Credit card, Retirement and pensions, financial inclusion schemes by government, Fraud protection and grievance redressel. This program is initiated by National Centre for Financial Education (NCFE).

Financial Education Programme for Adults (FEPA) create awareness among financially excluded people of various organization, Self help groups, Farmer, Rural people, MNREGA worker and other financially excluded sections of the society. The workshop conducted by NCFE and it is totally free of cost.

5.2 Financial Education Training Program (FETP):- Financial Education Training Program is an initiative by NCFE to provide training of school teachers of Class 8 to 10 across India and after completion of training certified them as a "Money Smart Teacher". The Teacher would conduct financial education classes in schools and encourages them about financial services and need.

The motto of this program is to establish a sustainable financial education that can empower people in every aspect of financial services.

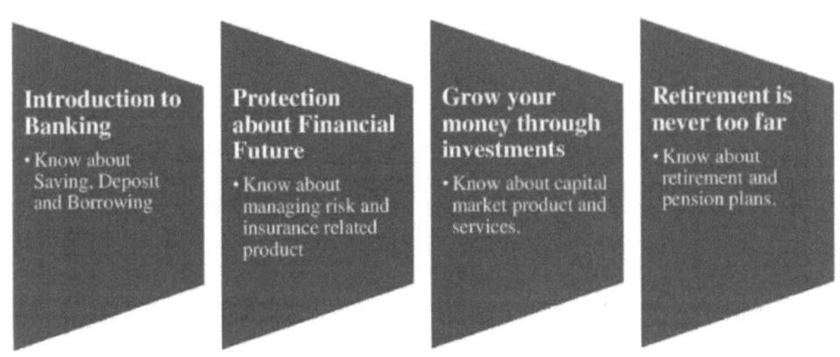

Modules of FETP

5.3 Financial Awareness and Consumer Training (FACT):- India has a large number of young populations and in order to make them financially included we need to provide training about financial literacy. Financial Awareness and Consumer Training (FACT) is a training program for young graduates and post graduates on financial topics which is relevant for them and help them in rational financial decision makers. FACT helps young people to set financial goals, financial, take financial obligations and aware them about rights and responsibilities of financial consumers.

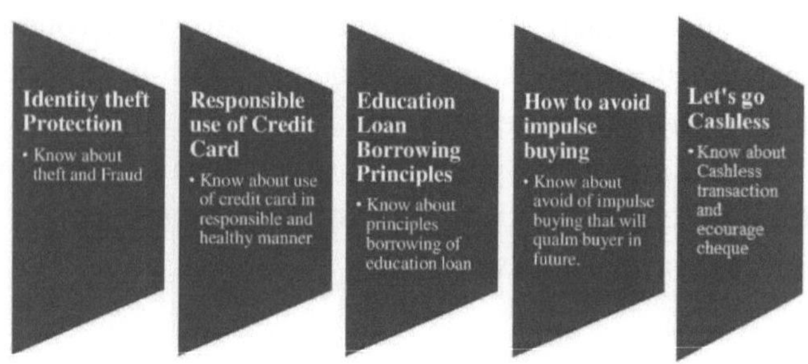

Modules of FACT

5.4 Money Smart School Program (MSSP):- Money Smart School Program (MSSP) is an initiative by NCFE to provide financial education in a school for improving financial literacy among students and provide skills and holistic development of each student.

The motto of MSSP is to provide financial products and services in today's complex environment and helps them in money management.

5.5 Initiative taken by RBI on Financial Literacy:- (RBI, 2017)

Financial Inclusion and Financial Education are two facets of the Reserve Bank of India's developmental mission. To this aim, the RBI has created a few infographics, handbooks, pamphlets, and other materials that are accessible on its website in approximately 13 languages and can be downloaded by financial institutions and other institutions for use in educating the public about financial goods and services. RBI created the booklet FAME to help the general population learn the basics of financial literacy (Financial Awareness Messages).

To raise awareness about issues like "Basic Financial Literacy," "Unified Payments Interface," and "Going Digital," audiovisuals have also been made. The Reserve Bank's "Raju" and "Money Kumar" series of pictures were equally successful ones. The booklets "Raju" and "Money Kumar" explained the role and duties of the Reserve Bank of India. "Raju" taught about banking ideas and saving practices.

The RBI's financial literacy programme greatly benefits from the "Project Financial Literacy" initiative. This project's goal is to inform diverse target groups on the concepts of universal banking and the RBI. In addition to this, RBI also hosts town hall meetings and outreach events in which all the top executives participate and share knowledge about the economy, banking, and RBI.

5.6 Initiatives taken by SEBI on Financial Literacy: (SEBI, 2017)

The Indian Securities Exchange Board has carried out financial education programmes through a national wide campaign has been formed by SEBI. SEBI has established the National Institutes of securities markets (NISM), which was established to increase the financial literacy of people from all backgrounds. Additionally, NISM has been running an Investor Education Program. Financial literacy tests are administered by NISM, and Pocket financial education classes are offered in schools every year. Resource Persons have been nominated by SEBI, and they schooled and prepared with an understanding of the financial markets for implementing investor education programmes around the country. They were chosen to provide financial literacy instruction to people from different social groups.

Financial market intermediaries like stock exchanges, depositories, the Association of Mutual Funds in India, the Association of Merchant Bankers of India, etc. are also checked out by SEBI.

Students from various educational institutions are urged to visit SEBI and become familiar with its activities through the "Visit SEBI" programme. Investors around the nation can file complaints and have their problems resolved through the SEBI Helpline and SCORES (SEBI Online Complaint Redressal System).

5.7 Initiatives taken by IRDA on Financial Education:

In the area of financial literacy, the Insurance Regulatory and Development Authority has also undertaken a variety of projects. Through the National Strategy for Financial Education, frequent awareness campaigns have been held to provide information on the rights and obligations of policyholders, the channels available for dispute and grievance redressal, etc (NSFE). Through a variety of communication means, including television, radio, print media, and others, these messages have been broadcast throughout the nation in several Indian languages. IRDAI has also taken part in the Ministry of Consumer Affairs, Food and Public Distribution of India's "JAGO GRAHAK JAGO" consumer education initiative.

The consumer education effort "Promoting Insurance Protecting Insured" (Bima Bemisaal), run by the Insurance Regulatory and Development Authority (IRDA), raises knowledge of insurance among the general people. IRDA has developed an integrated grievance management system (IGMS) that serves as a central repository for complaints and makes it easier for policyholders to register complaints and follow the case's development.

The NCAER was used to conduct the survey on insurance awareness levels, which IRDA used to refine its approach for raising insurance knowledge. The IRDA offers numerous insurance-related seminars as well as ones on the welfare and protection of policyholders. Similar to RBI, IRDA has released "Policyholder Handbooks" and an insurance-related comic book series. For the purpose of educating policyholders, IRDA has also launched the website www.policyholder.gov.in.

5.8 Initiatives taken by NCFE National Council of Financial Education:-

To improve financial literacy and financial inclusion in India, the National Centre for Financial Education (NCFE) was established with the support of the financial sector regulators, including the Reserve Bank of India (RBI), Securities and Exchange Board of India (SEBI), Insurance Regulatory and Development Authority (IRDA), and additional support from Pension Fund Regulatory and Development Authority (PFRDA) and Forward Markets Commission (FMC).

Every year, NCFE administers the National Financial Literacy Assessment Test (NFLAT), which is intended for students in Classes VIII through X. This exam aids students in developing their financial literacy during the academic year.

CHAPTER SIX

FINANCIAL LITERACY AND THE FINANCIAL WELLBEING

6.1 Financial Wellbeing:

Financial literacy is said to be a crucial factor in enabling people to compare financial products and services and to make sensible, well-informed financial decisions. Consumers can handle financial concerns more confidently and respond to news and events that could affect their financial well-being if they have a basic understanding of financial concepts and the capacity to apply numeracy abilities in a financial context.

The same report notes that customers' choices and behaviour have a significant impact on how well they can manage their finances. A person's financial condition and well-being may be severely impacted by certain behaviours, such as failing to actively save money, delaying payment of bills, failing to budget for future expenses, and selecting financial products without doing any comparison shopping.

Financial literacy is defined as "a combination of awareness, knowledge, skills, attitudes, and behaviour necessary to make sound financial decisions and ultimately achieve individual financial well-being" by the Organization for Economic Cooperation and Development/International Network on Financial Education (OECD/INFE). This acknowledges that a person's attitudes will affect whether they decide to act, even if they have the knowledge and skills necessary to do so. According to this concept, the purpose of financial education is also to increase financial literacy, which will allow people to improve their financial well-being.

6.2 Financial Literacy and Financial Wellbeing: A Review

Every person tries to improve his financial situation better and, in the end, to achieve financial well-being. When someone is financially well-off, they have less financial stress and are in a state of financial happiness.

(Rahmani, Nayebzadeh, & Addin, 2013)studied the link between financial knowledge, financial wellbeing, and financial concerns. Age, gender, marital status, level of education, and other demographic factors were examined to see how they would affect financial literacy, financial well-being, and financial concern. The correlation, T test, and regression analysis showed that there was a positive association between age and gender and the financial literacy and well-being variables. Financial literacy and financial well-being were found to be favorably impacted by education. Additionally, it was discovered that greater financial well-being was accompanied by good levels of financial knowledge, and that greater financial literacy reduced financial worries.

(Russell, Kutin, Green, Banks, & Iorio, 2016)believed that institutional, interpersonal, and individual factors all play an important role in one's financial well-being. They believed that gender experience is deeply imbedded in these fields. They discovered that a complex web of circumstances that affect a woman's personal financial decisions are developed by the social structure, families, and interpersonal interactions. Thus, their research supports the idea that gender must be considered as more than just a trait but rather as a factor that significantly influences both financial decision-making and well-being.

(Arellano, Cámara, & Tuesta, 2014) used information from the OECD's 2012 report on financial literacy from the Programme for International Student Assessment (PISA). The study's target audience were Spanish youth. Through financial literacy analysis, they examined young people's self-confidence affected their financial capabilities. The study investigates how non-cognitive elements affect financial literacy. The findings showed that individuals with higher degrees of financial literacy also had higher levels of confidence. Personal attitudes were found to affect financial behaviour patterns as well. Financial well-being was found to be enhanced by self-assurance, but it was also observed that overconfidence would result in a decline in wellbeing. Four aspects of self-confidence were examined: first, the student's self-confidence in their study environment, second, the usefulness of school, third, the outcomes of the financial literacy test, and fourth, self-confidence in a broader sense. Ultimately, it was found that elements other than an individual's interest traits affect financial literacy, including maturity, gender, socioeconomic features, and the environment.

(Bowman, Banks, Fela, Russell, & Silva, 2017) developed a foundation for a more comprehensive understanding of the elements that influence financial well-being and give people the tools to enjoy economic security. Financial inclusion, literacy, and the capacity for resilience and wellbeing in the new era are the main points of emphasis. The researchers emphasized that financial security is a current concern and is well-liked in the interrelated sectors of social policy, service provision, and personal financial products. Financial well-being can help us grasp economic security and social cohesion more fully as a part of overall wellbeing. According to the researchers, financial wellness now faces challenging conceptual issues; as a result, a framework that would contain concepts that center on the social arena as its main unit of analysis has to be built. Thus, Financial management, saving motivations, and financial literacy were found to be significantly correlated with financial wellbeing. Overall, age was a significant predictor of women's financial wellbeing. Financial wellbeing was also significantly influenced by the desire to save.

CHAPTER SEVEN

Challenges, Mechanism and Conclusion

7.1 Challenges of financial Literacy:

The problems with banks of developing country is that it must overcome in order to contribute to the improvement of living standards, support local economic development, and foster greater social cohesion at the local level are fundamental to their identity and one of their defining characteristics among other financial players. The greater commitment made by savings banks to the communities in which they operate includes financial education. The direct influence and tangible benefits that having a bank account or better budgeting or financial planning can have on clients should be a priority for banks.

Because they do not have access to many formal financial institutions like banks, insurance firms, and social security programmes, poor people, like everyone else, are at a disadvantage.

This is helpful in spreading fundamental knowledge about responsible consumption, the dangers of (easy) credit, and very concrete examples regarding saving. Given that many lower-income customers do not have bank accounts, there is also worry that these consumers are not adequately equipped to make wise financial decisions (due to a lack of knowledge and experience with personal finance and consumer education ideas).

Basic education and financial literacy have been neglected due to a lack of political will on the part of the administration. As a result, basic education and financial literacy have received little funding and have been seen as an aside in financial organizations' strategies. It takes a lot of work to increase financial competence through schooling. Reaching people at crucial periods in their lives presents a major challenge due to the diversity and complexity of their talents and demands. Other developments draw attention to the possibly unfavorable ways that people are managing their finances. Some families opt to lease their cars rather than buy them, which leaves them with less assets and a never-ending car payment obligation.

Therefore, one of the challenges is persuading the government and financial institutions to place a high value on the development of their citizens' financial literacy and to design policies in collaboration with social partners and other stakeholders to support the promotion of fundamental financial literacy education.

7.2 Mechanism to increase financial literacy:-

Financial inclusion and financial literacy are one of the two pillars of inclusive growth. Financial inclusion act as a supply side i.e what people demand from the financial market whereas financial literacy acts as a demand side i.e making people aware about financial services. Financial literacy is equally important not only for investors and but also for common man to identify the money management in day-to-day activities. Hence, a well-developed financial system could bring poor people into mainstream of the economy and allows them to contribute in country's economic development.

7.2.1 Introducing Financial literacy in primary school curriculum:- Providing financial educations from young age should be a significant improvement is overall budgeting behavior. Thus, financial education must be integrated into school curriculum so that young population from developing countries like India should be aware and financially sound. Recently CBSE and NPCI have joined hands to introduce financial education at early stage. The curriculum has started as a elective course from class 6th and beyond. The textbooks cover information regarding financial behavior like Concepts of banking, UPI, Debit cards, Credit cards, Digital payments and more. The textbook also covers the role of RBI and GoI in expanding financial services. So, the new policy should stress on the basic financial concepts with ease and establishes sound financial decision for the new generations.

7.2.2 Collaboration of Public and Private sector:- Financial literacy is one of the agenda for Indian government. Although National strategy for financial inclusion is set up to provide broader and long-term guidelines for upcoming five year NSFE (2020-2025). There is also need to collect periodic data of demand and supply side access to finance for the policymaking. In this position private players should play a vital role in data collection and analyzing. So, therefore public and private sectors should closely work together in maximizing the use of new technology for enhances access to finance.

7.2.3 Digitization and Artificial Intelligence (AI):- The collaborative role of digitization and AI as the new key catalysts for increasing financial education in the countries like India where majority of population is still unaware about financial services. In an interactive session of financial literacy in DAV united festival 2020, Rohit gajbhiye, a founder of fintech company 'financepeer' has stressed the role of digitization and AI. He has said improving financial literacy is a multi-dimensional approach and persistent action over it can make changes in it. He has further told that AI can facilitate dealing with finances and financial institutions more effective and take away the stigma and fear around the dealing of money. Thus financial literacy can improve with the help of digitization and AI in the lower income group countries like India where usage of internet data services is cheap.

7.2.4 One sized fit programmes:- Financial education programmes is an effective tools for financial literacy. India is a land of diversity of people, the diversity in terms of language, culture, and income levels too. So, financial education should avoid one-size-fits programmes and target different segments differently. In India, financial education needs to move away from designing programmes for one sections of society. For example, designing programmes for middle class individuals should be avoided because middle class have reached a stable ground and ready to save. So, therefore in India, each programme should be made for each sections of the society. Youths are the largest beneficiary in India and many more programmes should be made for creating awareness among the youth.

7.2.5 Collaboration of Educational institutions with Industry bodies:- In many western countries educational institutions are linked with industry to strengthen the need of job creation, financial literacy and empowering the investors. So, in India educational institutions, think tanks, stakeholders and research institutions should come forward to increase the responsibility of inclusive growth. This will also increase the financial literacy through proper collaborations. Collaboration between different stakeholders in our country increases and promotes investor awareness, education and protection.

7.2.6 Increase General Literacy:- Low literacy level among the populations are also a major hindrances in increasing financial literacy. Traditionally literacy means ability to write and read and according to these parameters every fourth India's population is illiterate. According to traditionally only 75% of India's population is literate. But in the world of digital communications only 38% of India's households are digitally literate. In urban areas digital literacy is 61% and just 25% in rural India's. So, due to limited exposure and knowledge of communications, people are reluctant in the activities and programmes. Hence there is urgent need to improve general literacy among the population to improve financial literacy.

7.3 Conclusion:

The economic transformation of a nation can be greatly accelerated by the proper implementation of financial inclusion as a complete development strategy. The impact and reachability of the policy's objectives must be thoroughly examined from the policy maker's standpoint.

Numerous programmes for financial inclusion targeting different demographic groups. Studying the effects of such initiatives on the women folk, who make up half the population of our country, is even more important in light of the existence of gender specific constraints leading to policy paralysis in the case of many development measures. The multi-faceted process of financial inclusion for women is influenced by a wide range of variables, which were divided into economic, sociocultural, technological, and geographic elements. It identified the main perceived supply-side and demand-side barriers to increased financial inclusion for women. Corrective action should be performed from an institutional standpoint with regard to the risk-averse mindset of banking authorities, complicated banking processes, geographical limitations, acceptability of financial goods and services, etc. On the supply side, policy interventions should be started to improve women's employment and income status, uphold their legal rights to inherit and own assets, properties, and other resources, equip them with the tools they need to be financially independent, and raise their level of financial literacy. Lack of decision-making power, low self-esteem, the load of domestic duties, a lack of social networks, etc. prevent many women from participating in the dynamic economy outside of their homes. Massive financial education campaigns, expanding agency banking and technology into rural areas, creating financial products and services specifically for women customers, using vernacular languages in banking procedures, gathering and analysing gender-disaggregated data, etc., all play crucial roles in effectively removing barriers to women's financial inclusion. For women to be able to hold real assets and hence improve their status as financial inclusion, income production through state-subsidized employment opportunities and formal bank credit is essential. To be more sustainable, financial literacy policies need to be improved in several ways, including coverage expansion, quality improvement, utilizing cutting-edge technology, increasing financial literacy, boosting financial capability, reinforcing institutional reformation, etc.

References

References, Websites, Webliography:-

1. Arellano, A., Cámara, N., & Tuesta, D. (2014). The effect of self-confidence on financial literacy. *BBVA Research WP*, *14*(28), 1-25.
2. India, T. (2020, August 21). Financial Literacy in India: Jan dhan yojana boosts financial literacy to 27%: India Business News - Times of India. Retrieved February 3, 2022, from https://timesofindia.indiatimes.com/business/india-business/jan-dhan-yojana-boosts-financial-literacy-to-27/articleshow/77663200.cms
3. Atkinson, A., & Messy, F. A. (2012). Measuring financial literacy: Results of the OECD/International Network on Financial Education (INFE) pilot study.
4. Anthes, W. L. (2004). Financial Illiteracy in America: A Perfect Storm, a Perfect Opportunity. *Journal of Financial Service Professionals*, 58(6).
5. Atkinson, A., & Kempson, E. (2004). Young people, money management, borrowing and saving. *A Report to the Banking Code Standard.*
6. Bowman, D., Banks, M., Fela, G., Russell, R., & de Silva, A. (2017). Understanding financial wellbeing in times of insecurity.
7. Bernheim, B. D., & Garrett, D. M. (2003). The effects of financial education in the workplace: Evidence from a survey of households. *Journal of public Economics*, *87*(7-8), 1487-1519.
8. Creevey, L., & Edgerton, J. (1997). Evaluation of the impacts of grassroots management training on women in India. *Canadian Journal of Development Studies/Revue*

canadienne d'études du développement, *18*(sup1), 645-672.

9. Clancy, M., Grinstein-Weiss, M., & Schreiner, M. (2001). Financial education and savings outcomes in individual development accounts.
10. Collaborative, W. B. *8.2% of Fortune 500 CEOs are Women, According to the 2021 Women CEOs in America Report*. Www.prnewswire.com. https://www.prnewswire.com/news-releases/8-2-of-fortune-500-ceos-are-women-according-to-the-2021-women-ceos-in-america-report-301400856.html
11. Chen, H., & Volpe, R. P. (1998). An analysis of personal financial literacy among college students. *Financial services review*, 7(2), 107-128.
12. Duflo, E., & Saez, E. (2003). The role of information and social interactions in retirement plan decisions: Evidence from a randomized experiment. *The Quarterly journal of economics*, *118*(3), 815-842.
13. Financial Literacy Initiative undertaken by Securities and Exchange Board of India (SEBI). Retrieved October 27, 2022, from https://www.ncfe.org.in/financial-literacy-initiative-undertaken-by-sebi
14. *Financial Literacy Initiative undertaken by Insurance Regulatory and Development Authority of India (IRDAI)*. (n.d.). https://www.pfrda.org.in/writereaddata/links/
15. *GLOBAL GENDER GAP REPORT*. (2021). Pib.gov.in.https://pib.gov.in/PressReleaseIframePage.aspx?PRID=1782628
16. *Global Gender Gap Report*. (2017). https://www3.weforum.org/docs/WEF_GGGR_2021.pdf
17. Gupta, S. (2015, December 15). *76% Indians not*

financially literate, says S&P survey - Times of India. The Times of India. https://timesofindia.indiatimes.com/business/india-business/76-indians-not-financially-literate-says-sp-survey/articleshow/50184941.cms

18. Kim, J., & Garman, E. T. (2004). Financial stress, pay satisfaction and workplace performance. *Compensation Benefits Review*, 36(1), 69-76.
19. Group, T. Q. (2017, March 13). *Financial Facts for Women's History Month.* The Quantum Group. https://thequantum.com/financial-facts-for-womens-history-month/
20. Hung, A., Yoong, J., & Brown, E. (2012). Empowering women through financial awareness and education.
21. Hathaway, I., & Khatiwada, S. (2008). Do financial education programs work?
22. Halder, S. R., & Mosley, P. (2004). Working with the ultra-poor: learning from BRAC experiences. *Journal of International Development*, *16*(3), 387-406.
23. Hogarth J, O'Donnell KH (1997). Being Accountable: A Descriptive Study of Unbanked Households in the U.S. Proceedings of the Association for Financial Counseling and Planning Education, Phoenix, Arizona.
24. *Jump$tart Coalition: Financial Smarts for Students.* Jump$Tart Coalition. https://www.jumpstart.org/
25. Jacob K, Sharyl H, Malcolm B (2000). Tools for Survival: An Analysis of Financial Literacy Programs For Lower-Income Families http://www.woodstockinst.org/document/toolsforsurvival.pdf.
26. Rohde, J. (1997). *Rich Dad Poor Dad - A Quick Book Summary and Review.* Learn.roofstock.com. https://learn.roofstock.com/blog/rich-dad-poor-dad-summary
27. Rutherford S (2000). The Poor and their Money. New

Delhi: Oxford University Press.

28. Klapper, L., Lusardi, A., & Van Oudheusden, P. (2015). *Financial Literacy Around the World: INSIGHTS FROM THE STANDARD & POOR'S RATINGS SERVICES GLOBAL FINANCIAL LITERACY SURVEY.* https://gflec.org/wp-content/uploads/2015/11/3313-Finlit_Report_FINAL-5.11.16.pdf
29. Klapper, L., Singer, D., & Bank, W. (2017). *The role of demand-side data -measuring financial inclusion from the perspective of users of financial services 1.* https://www.bis.org/ifc/publ/ifcb47o.pdf
30. Kempson, E., & Collard, S. (2010). Money Guidance Pathfinder-A Report to the FSA.
31. Lusardi, A., & Mitchell, O. S. (2014). The economic importance of financial literacy: Theory and evidence. *American Economic Journal: Journal of Economic Literature, 52*(1), 5-44.
32. Kidwell, B., & Turrisi, R. (2004). An examination of college student money management tendencies. *Journal of Economic Psychology,* 25(5), 601-616.
33. *Measuring Financial Literacy: Questionnaire and Guidance Notes for Conducting an Internationally Comparable Survey of Financial Literacy.* (n.d.). https://www.oecd.org/finance/financial-education/49319977.pdf
34. *NSFE 2020-25.* (n.d.). Ncfe.org.in. Retrieved February 27, 2022, from https://ncfe.org.in/reports/nsfe/nsfe2025
35. NCFE. *Initiatives taken by NCFE National Council of Financial Education:-.* https://www.ncfe.org.in/financial-literacy-initiative-undertaken-by-ncfe
36. OECD. (2020). *OECD/INFE 2020 International Survey of Adult Financial Literacy.* https://www.oecd.org/

financial/education/oecd-infe-2020-international-survey-of-adult-financial-literacy.pdf

37. Office, U. S. G. A. *Financial Literacy and Education Commission: Further Progress Needed to Ensure an Effective National Strategy*. Www.gao.gov. Retrieved January 22, 2022, from https://www.gao.gov/products/gao-07-777t
38. Organization for Economic Co-Operation and Development. 2005. Improving Financial Literacy: Analysis of Issues and Policies.
39. Quelvog, O. D. Financial Coaching in the Corps: Reducing Stress of Junior Marines.
40. Rana, R. (2021, December 17). *The Importance Of Financial Literacy: Why It Needs To Be Included In Our Education System?* Thelogicalindian.com. https://thelogicalindian.com/education/financial-literacy-32666
41. *Reserve Bank of India - Reports*. Www.rbi.org.in. https://www.rbi.org.in/Scripts/PublicationReportDetails.aspx?UrlPage=&ID=1156
42. RBI. Financial Literacy Initiative undertaken by Reserve Bank of India (RBI). Retrieved October 27, 2022, from https://www.ncfe.org.in/financial-literacy-initiative-undertaken-by-rbi
43. Rahmani, A., Nayebzadeh, S., & Addin, M. M. (2013). Investigation of the effects of accounting teachers demographic characteristics on their attitude about acceptable behavior in the role of teacher and researcher. *Advances in Environmental Biology*, *7*(10 S1), 2782-2789.
44. Russell, R., Kutin, J., Green, R., Banks, M., & Di Iorio, A. (2016). Women and money in Australia: Across the generations.

45. Tezel, Z. (2015). Financial Education for Children and Youth. *Handbook Of Research On Behavioral Finance And Investment Strategies,* 69-92. doi: 10.4018/978-1-4666-7484- 4.ch005
46. The World Bank. (2020). *Life expectancy at birth, total (years) | Data.* Worldbank.org. https://data.worldbank.org/indicator/SP.DYN.LE00.IN
47. *Worldbank Search.* (n.d.). Www.worldbank.org. Retrieved January 27, 2022, from https://www.worldbank.org/en/search?q=Financial+literacy

9 798889 595410

Printed by Libri Plureos GmbH in Hamburg, Germany